COMMUNICATING BY SIGNS

RUPERT MATTHEWS

SIGNS & SYMBOLS ➤

Body Language
Codes and Ciphers
Communicating by Signs
Writing and Numbers

Cover: Two deaf people, communicating in sign language.

First published in 1990 by
Wayland (Publishers) Ltd.
61 Western Road, Hove
East Sussex BN3 1JD, England

© Copyright 1990 Wayland (Publishers) Ltd.

Series Originator: Theodore Rowland-Entwistle
Series Editor: Mike Hirst
Series Designer: Michael Morey

British Library Cataloguing in Publication Data
Matthews, Rupert
   Communicating by signs.
   1. Communication
   I. Title
   302.2

HARDBACK ISBN 1–85210–887–8

PAPERBACK ISBN 0–7502–0578–4

Typeset by Nicola Taylor, Wayland
Printed and bound in Italy by
L.E.G.O. S.p.A., Vicenza.

CONTENTS

All the words that appear in **bold** are explained in the glossary on page 30.

ROAD SIGNS

Can you think of all the different ways in which you communicate with other people? You might use speech and communicate by talking to someone. Or you can communicate by writing. In both speech and writing you would be using words.

Yet words are not our only means of communication. Sometimes we need to pass on information in other ways. What would you do if you needed to say something to someone who could not speak your language? Or how would you write a message to someone who could not read? You would probably decide to use signs.

The road signs that you can see in any street are a good example of communicating by signs. These road signs give instructions to road users and also warn drivers about road **hazards**. When someone learns to drive a car, they must learn all the signs by heart. You should also know the road signs if you ride a bicycle.

This hazard warning sign in Sweden warns drivers that there may be elk on the road ahead.

Road signs are not exactly the same all over the world. For instance, in the USA, the speed limit is marked by black numbers on a white background, with the words 'Speed Limit' underneath. In Western Europe, the speed limit is shown in black numbers on a white background inside a red circle. However, road signs usually rely on pictures and simple diagrams rather than words. So you can often work out what the signs mean, even if you are in a foreign country and have never seen them before.

ROAD SIGNS AROUND THE WORLD

These road signs are from different countries in North America and Europe. Can you guess what they mean, even if you have never seen them before?

1
2
3
4
5
6
7
8

Turn to page 31 to find out how many you could work out.

COLOUR CODING

One simple way of communicating by signs is to use **colour coding**. Traffic lights, for instance, use three different colours to give instructions which everyone can recognize. A red light means 'stop', an amber light means 'prepare for a change', and a green light means 'go if the road is clear'.

There are many other simple uses of colour coding. Taps on a bath or a washbasin are often colour coded, red for hot and blue or green for cold. Can you think of any other similar examples which you might see every day?

Colour coding is also an important way of giving information

Left Traffic lights are one of the commonest ways of using different colours to give information or instructions.

Below If someone carries a white stick, it means that they are visually handicapped.

When architects design a building, they mark the different kinds of pipe, for water, electricity and so on, in different colours. This unusual building is the Pompidou Centre in Paris. The architects designed the building with all the pipes on the outside, painted in the same colours as they were marked on the plans.

about machines that work by electricity, such as refrigerators, stereos and lamps. The wires that supply the electric power have special colours. A wire's colour shows where it should go and what it is supposed to do.

Have you ever seen the inside of a plug? You should never try to look inside one yourself, but you might ask an adult to open a plug for you, first making sure that it is not connected to any electricity supply. You will see at least two wires. One wire is coloured brown. This is the live wire. The second wire is coloured blue and is called the neutral wire. There may also be a third wire, which is striped yellow and green and is called the earth wire. For the plug to work safely, each wire must be connected to the correct part of the plug. Without colour coding, it would be easy to mix up the different wires and cause a fire.

HERALDRY

During the **Middle Ages**, people in Europe developed a complicated system of communicating by signs. This system of communication is called **heraldry**.

At that time, battles were fought by knights wearing armour. They wore helmets that covered their faces and so it was difficult for them to recognize one another. To solve this problem, each knight painted a different design on his shield. These designs were the first heraldic coats of arms.

As time passed, the rules of heraldry became very complicated. The eldest son of a knight **inherited** the coat of arms of his father and used it as his own. Some of the coats of arms that are in use today date back hundreds of years. Some of the signs which were used on shields also had special meanings. For instance, a white bar across the top of the shield meant that the owner was the eldest son of a nobleman.

The system of heraldry did not always work. At the Battle of Barnet in 1471, the Earl of Warwick made a disastrous mistake. The shield of his friend, the Earl of Oxford, had a white star on it, and the shield of his enemy, the Duke of York, had a white rose. Warwick mixed up the two symbols, attacked his friend instead of his enemy and lost the battle.

Heraldry is still used today, and many countries have a national coat of arms. In the USA, each state also has its own coat of arms. These signs are used to mark state property, such as public buildings and cars or trucks.

Today, many towns throughout the world have their own coat of arms. This coat of arms belongs to the town of New Bern, in North Carolina, USA.

HERALDIC SYMBOLS

The different colours and shapes that are used in heraldry have special names.

The names of the heraldic colours:

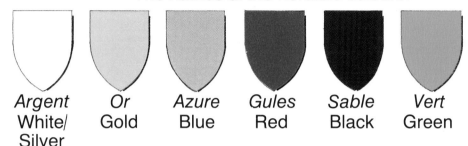

Argent	*Or*	*Azure*	*Gules*	*Sable*	*Vert*	*Purpure*
White/ Silver	Gold	Blue	Red	Black	Green	Purple

The names of some heraldic designs:

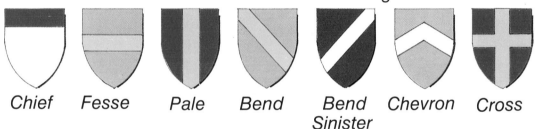

Chief	*Fesse*	*Pale*	*Bend*	*Bend Sinister*	*Chevron*	*Cross*

These special names are used to describe heraldic shields.
Here are two examples of shields with their descriptions:

Argent, a stag springing gules; on a chief vert three moles (stars) argent.

Argent, a chevron gules between three broad arrow heads, points upwards, sable.

BADGES

Lots of people wear badges. They often have a special design or **logo** and give all kinds of different messages. People may wear badges showing which political party they belong to. Some badges show that the wearer supports a campaign, to protect wildlife for instance. Other people may wear a badge to show that they belong to a particular club. Some people like wearing badges so they can be recognized by other members of the same group, who will know that they share the same interest or hobby.

Badges are specially important to Scouts and Guides. They can collect badges for learning new skills, such as cooking, swimming and first aid. They then sew the badges onto their uniforms.

Scouts and guides often have badges on their uniforms, showing the skills they have learnt.

MAKE YOUR OWN BADGE

You can make your own badge, with your own design and message drawn on it. It could be a serious badge, which shows your favourite pop star, or the football team you support. Or you could make a humorous badge with a motto such as 'Ban Homework' or 'Chocolate Appeal - Please Give Generously'. But you should be careful not to make a badge that might upset somebody.

You will need: Stiff card
                       Sticky tape
                       Safety pins
                       Crayons

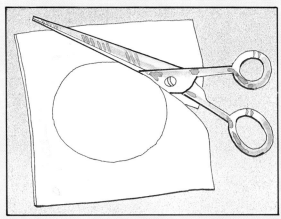

1 Cut out a circular piece of card in the correct size for your finished badge.

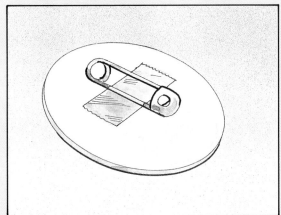

2 Draw a design and write a message on the card. Make your badge as bright and colourful as possible.

3 Attach the safety pin to the back of the badge with a piece of sticky tape. Now you can pin the badge to your shirt or jumper.

COMPANY LOGOS

The logo of the United Nations hangs on the wall of the organization's assembly chamber in New York.

Many modern companies and businesses use a special type of sign called a logo to communicate with the public. A logo is a symbol which stands for the company and can be easily recognized. The logo is put on all the company's products and can often be seen on advertisements as well. Logos help you to look out for products made by companies you like and that you know are good.

Some companies have very simple logos that include the name of the company. The computer company IBM, for instance, has a logo that is simply the letters IBM written in a special way. The oil company Shell uses a picture of a seashell with the word 'SHELL' written on it as its logo.

It is not only companies that use logos. For example, the Olympic Games, one of the biggest and most important sporting events in the world, has a logo of five **interlocking** circles. People from all over the world take part in the Olympic Games and the five circles stand for the five continents of the world.

Many charities and international organizations have logos too. The United Nations' logo consists of a picture of the earth, surrounded by two olive branches – a traditional sign for peace. There are many different groups within the United Nations, and each one has its own logo, based on the main design. The United Nations International Children's Fund (UNICEF), for instance, uses the shape of a mother holding a child, inside a **globe** surrounded by the two olive branches.

Above *The German car manufacturer, Mercedes Benz, has a logo which appears on all of the cars it makes.*

Left *The five interlocking circles which make up the Olympic logo.*

FLAGS

Every country has its own flag. These flags are signs that are recognized all over the world. They are an easy way of showing which country someone or something belongs to.

The first flags were used in wartime, like heraldic shields, so that troops could recognize their friends and enemies from a distance. Today, flags are also used for peaceful purposes. Every ship flies a flag showing the country to which it belongs. At sports meetings, such as the Olympic Games, each team carries its country's national flag. Important government buildings often fly flags, to mark that they belong to the whole country, not just to an individual person.

Some countries change their flags when the government changes. In 1917, the Russian Revolution established a new kind of government in Russia. To mark the Revolution, the new, **communist** leaders changed the name of their country to the Union of Soviet Socialist Republics (USSR), and introduced a new flag with a special meaning. The flag is red, a colour which stands for communism. On the red background are a hammer and a **sickle**, which are workers' tools. They showed that the new, communist government was to be run by the workers.

The flag of the USA is called the Stars and Stripes, and it has changed many times over the past two hundred years. The first flag was used when the United States was still a British **colony**. It had thirteen red and white stripes, one for each state, with the British Union Jack flag in the top left-hand

THE STARS AND STRIPES

As the USA has grown in size the Stars and Stripes has changed, with an extra star for each new state. These are three of the different versions of the flag.

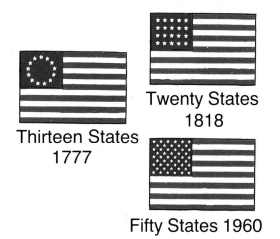

Twenty States 1818

Thirteen States 1777

Fifty States 1960

Flags from countries all over the world. How many can you recognize?

corner. When the United States became independent of Britain in 1777 it removed the Union Jack and replaced it with a circle of thirteen stars. Over the following years, the United States grew in size, and more states in North America became part of the nation. As new states joined the country, more stars were added to the flag, and today's flag has fifty stars, one for each of the states in the union.

THE UNION JACK

The British flag, the Union Jack, is made up of three other flags, from different parts of the British Isles. It is a combination of the flags of England, Scotland and Ireland. Can you see how they fit together?

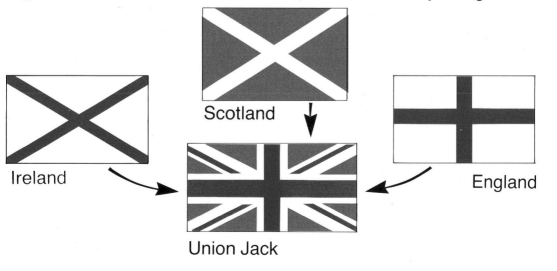

Scotland

Ireland

England

Union Jack

HAZARD SIGNS

Have you ever seen mysterious signs on a packing box or the side of a lorry? You might have spotted an unusual symbol such as a broken wineglass or a skull and crossbones and wondered what it meant. In fact, these signs are part of an international system, which helps people who transport goods from one place to another. The signs give important information about what is inside a container, and in some countries it is **illegal** to transport goods without the right signs attached to them.

The sign on these containers shows that they hold dangerous radioactive substances.

Goods labels tell people how to handle boxes and containers and also give warnings about any dangerous goods inside a package. For instance, if an object is fragile and may break easily, the sign of a broken wineglass is used. This sign tells the people carrying the package that they should be careful not to drop it. Sometimes packages also have large arrows to show which way up they should be carried.

Warning signs are even more important. A skull and crossbones tells everyone that the contents of a package are poisonous. If the contents catch fire easily, a red flame sign is put on the container. Strong chemicals are always transported in packages which carry a test-tube sign. There is also an international symbol for **radioactive** material, which can be very dangerous.

If a lorry is involved in an accident, these signs give vital information to the emergency services. Firefighters and ambulance crews need to know if there are any special dangers from spilt chemicals or explosive materials. The hazard warning signs tell them how to react and which equipment they should use.

DANGEROUS GOODS LABELS

Diamond-shaped symbols give information about dangerous substances. If you see a bottle or can which has one of these signs on the side, you should not open it or touch the contents.

Inflammable Gases

Toxic Gases

Compressed Gases

Inflammable Solids

Spontaneously Combustible Substances

Substances Which Are Dangerous When Wet

Oxidizing Substances

Harmful Substances - Keep Away From Food

Organic Peroxides

Poisonous Substances

Corrosive Substances

Radioactive Substances

TRACKING

Before the invention of radio, when many parts of the world had still not been explored and were not mapped, tracking signs were an important means of passing on information. If a large group of people, such as an army, wanted to travel across unknown territory, they had to use these signs to show one another the way.

All armies had scouts, who went ahead of the main troops. The scouts would work out the best route. They would then leave a trail of special signs for the rest of the army to follow. These signs were usually made from natural objects such as sticks and stones. Some peoples, such as native Americans, were expert at tracking in this way.

If you go tracking, you could leave signs such as this one, an arrow made of stone.

FOLLOWING A TRAIL

You can practise using tracking signs with a group of friends. First you should all agree about which signs you will use. You should copy these signs onto a sheet of paper.

Then choose an area, such as a playing field or a park. Two people set off, laying down the trail. They should try to make the course fairly short, but leaving as many signs as possible, so that the trail often changes direction. After a short while, the other people set off to follow the trail.

It can be fun to practise tracking if you go out for a picnic. Two people go on ahead and lay a trail leading to the food. The others set off later, following the signs until they catch up with their friends and the picnic.

Here are some suggestions for tracking signs:

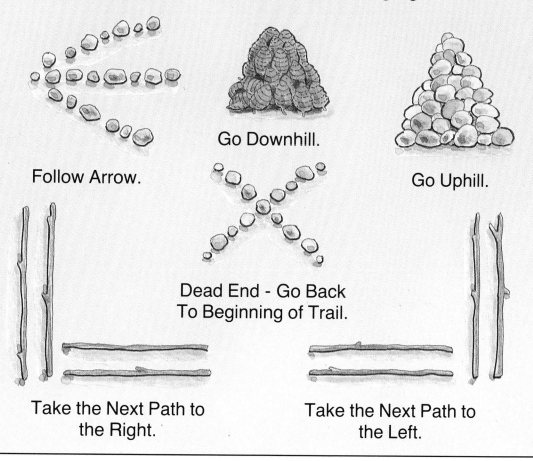

Follow Arrow.

Go Downhill.

Go Uphill.

Dead End - Go Back
To Beginning of Trail.

Take the Next Path to
the Right.

Take the Next Path to
the Left.

GRAPHS

Signs sometimes show information much more clearly than words. Often, one of the simplest ways of putting across complicated facts and figures is to draw a graph. If you have a **protractor,** you can make up the kind of graph below, called a pie chart.

MAKE A PIE CHART

You could make a pie chart to show the shoe colours of all the people in your class at school. The chart will look rather like a pie cut into different sized pieces. The pie chart will make it easy to see how big a share of the class wears each size of shoe.

You will need: A compass
A pencil
A protractor
Coloured pencils

1 First, ask everyone what colour shoes they wear, and write down the information. You might get results like this:

SHOE COLOUR	NUMBER OF PEOPLE WITH THAT COLOUR OF SHOE
Dark Brown	7
Light Brown	6
Black	4
Red	5
Blue	11
Green	3
TOTAL	**36**

Add up the total number of people in your class. In this case it is 36.

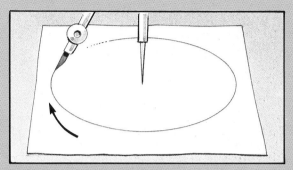

2 Using a compass, draw a large circle on a piece of paper.

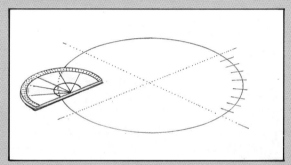

3 A circle is divided into degrees. There are 360 degrees in a circle, and they are measured with a protractor. You need to work out how much of the circle belongs to each person. To do this divide 360 (the number of degrees in the circle) by 36 (the number of people in the class).

360° ÷ 36 = 10°

In this case, each person has a 10° share.

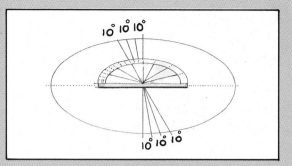

4 Using the protractor, divide the circle into 10° segments with a light pencil line.

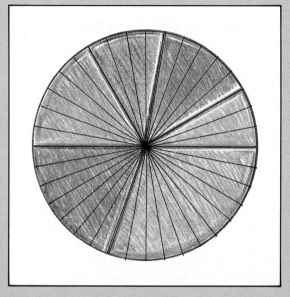

5 Choose a coloured pencil for each shoe colour. Then shade in the correct number of segments for each of the different shoe colours. In this pie chart, seven segments will be dark brown, six segments will be light brown and so on.

A pie chart like this one makes it easy to see how big a share of the class wears each colour of shoe.

SHORTHAND

Have you ever wished that you could write really quickly? Over the centuries, many people have felt that ordinary writing was too slow for them. So they have developed new ways of writing, in which the normal letters of the alphabet are replaced with signs and symbols. These ways of writing quickly are called shorthand.

People began to find ways of writing quickly as long ago as Roman times, and many famous authors have used shorthand. Shakespeare's plays were first written down in shorthand. Samuel Pepys, who lived in London in the seventeenth century, wrote a famous diary in shorthand.

The form of shorthand which is probably most widely used today is called Pitman Shorthand, and was invented by Sir Isaac Pitman (1813–97). This system replaces the letters of the alphabet with much simpler signs and pen strokes. Unlike ordinary writing, all words are written as they sound (so, for instance, the words bare and bear are written in the same way.) Isaac Pitman also thought of a clever way of showing the **vowel** sounds in words. In some words the vowel is missed out altogether,

Pitman Shorthand is usually written with a pencil, not an ink pen. A thick, heavy pencil line can have a different meaning from a light, thin line.

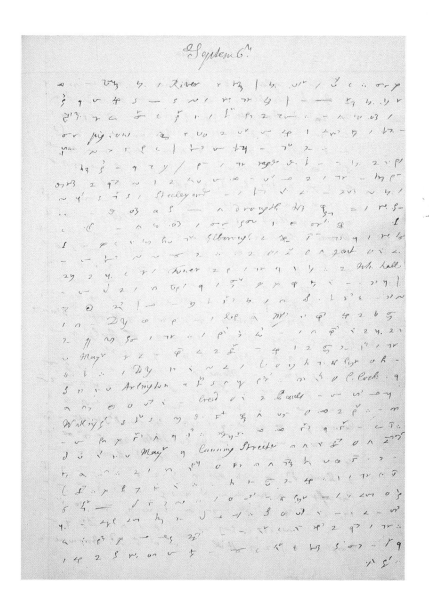

A page from a diary of Samuel Pepys. He wrote in a mixture of ordinary writing and his own, secret shorthand.

but the position of the word, either above, resting on or below the line tells you what the vowel should be.

In addition to Pitman, there are other popular forms of shorthand, such as Gregg and Teeline shorthand. One type of shorthand, called Speedwriting, is very easy to learn because it uses a mixture of special signs and ordinary letters of the alphabet.

Many people use shorthand every day as part of their work and it is not unusual for people to write shorthand as quickly as they speak, at 140 or 150 words per minute. Most secretaries know shorthand and in law courts, the details of each trial are recorded in it. Journalists often learn shorthand too, so that they can write down exactly what people say.

FIRE SIGNALS

On a clear, dark night, even a small light can be seen for a surprisingly long distance. Before the invention of radio and telephones, fire signals were often used to pass information over long distances.

One of the most famous examples of signalling using fire took place in England in 1588.

England was at war with Spain, and the Spanish had launched a fleet of ships to attack and invade England. The English built bonfires on the tops of hills throughout the country, and posted watchmen to stand by them all the time. Then, when the Spanish Armada was sighted from the south coast, the

A statue of Paul Revere in Boston, USA. It marks the spot from which Revere set off on his famous ride.

This painting, by the American artist, Frederic Remington, shows native American people during the last century sending smoke signals.

first bonfire was lit. When the fire was seen by the next watchman in the chain, he lit his fire. In this way the message passed quickly through the whole country, and although the Spanish were defeated at sea and never actually landed in England, everyone was alerted to the possible danger.

Fire signals were also important during the American Revolution, when the American colonies were fighting for their independence from the British. In 1775, a force of British soldiers in Boston was ordered to capture a store of ammunition owned by American **patriots** in the nearby town of Concord. An American patriot, named Paul Revere, who lived in Boston, was to watch the British and see if they approached Concord by the road or the river. If they went on the road, Revere was to light one lantern in the church steeple, but if they came by the river he was to light two lanterns. On the night of 18 April, the British left Boston by road. Revere lit one lantern in the steeple and then set off on horseback to round up American soldiers to stop the British. The Americans saw the signal and managed to stop the British attack.

Fires can also be used to make smoke signals in daylight. The native people of North America were famous for this method of signalling. They used blankets to control how much smoke left a fire, and produced small puffs of smoke which had a special, pre-arranged meaning, like Paul Revere's lanterns. **25**

A LANGUAGE FOR DEAF PEOPLE

For people who are deaf, signs are a vitally important way of communicating. Within the deaf community, people have developed a very complex system of sign language, which is used in place of spoken language.

Signs and **gestures** are the most natural way for deaf people to communicate with one another. Wherever groups of deaf people have lived together, they have probably always worked out their own sign language. However, it

*The French priest who pioneered sign language, Charles de l'Epée (**left**), and a church service specially for deaf people held in sign language during the nineteenth century (**below**).*

A travel agent who specializes in selling holidays to deaf people. He is using sign language to communicate with a customer.

was not until the eighteenth century that hearing people began to recognize this language.

One of the pioneers of this sign language was a French priest, Charles de l'Epée (1712–1789). He first began to understand sign language when he met deaf twin sisters, who communicated with each other in a very elaborate system of gestures. He set up a small school for deaf children, which later became the National Institute for Deaf and Dumb People in Paris. At this school, modern sign language was developed.

In sign language, the words of spoken language are replaced by hand and arm movements and facial expressions. Different words are also made up using different hand shapes. Some examples of words and phrases in sign language are shown on the following pages.

Sign language is not the only way in which deaf people communicate. Like hearing people, they must learn to read and write and many deaf people can also understand spoken language by lip reading. But sign language often seems to be the most natural way for deaf people to communicate. Have you ever seen anyone using sign language? There have been television programmes and even plays in which the characters 'speak' in sign language. You might also have seen a sign language interpreter at a conference or large meeting, translating a speech into sign language for deaf members of the audience.

SIGN LANGUAGES

Some of the signs in sign language are clear and easy to understand, though other signs are not quite so obvious. For hearing people, learning sign language is just like learning a foreign language, and there are many different words and phrases which need to be memorized.

There are also different kinds of sign language in different countries, in just the same way that hearing people speak a variety of languages. So in Germany, German sign language is used, while in France, people learn French sign language and in Denmark, Danish sign language and so on. There are also two kinds of sign language used in Britain and North America. In Britain, Canada and the USA, hearing people speak the same language, English. But deaf people in North America use American Sign Language (ASL), while British deaf people use British Sign Language (BSL). As you can see from the illustrations on the opposite page, some of the words in these two languages are quite different.

The signal for 'Hello' in sign language. The signer moves their hand in an arc shape as though they were waving.

MAKING SIGNS

These are some of the gestures used in sign language. Can you make these signs yourself?

These are two signs for animals:

FISH

DOG

Left *This sign-language phrase means, 'What is your name?' You can tell that the boy is asking a question by the 'questioning' expression on his face.*

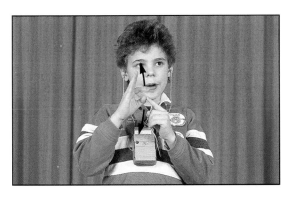

Above *These two signs both have the same meaning – 'paper'. The sign on the left is part of British Sign Language and the sign on the right is American Sign Language.*

GLOSSARY

Colony   A settlement of people in a new country.

Colour coding   Giving a special meaning to a colour, such as blue standing for cold.

Communist   Someone who believes that industry and agriculture should be controlled by the government so that the wealth of a country can be shared out fairly amongst everyone.

Gestures   Signs made by the hands, or facial expressions.

Globe   A round ball, the shape of the earth.

Hazard   A risk or danger.

Heraldry   The system of signs on coats of arms.

Illegal   Against the law.

Inherited   Received as a gift from someone who has died.

Interlocking   Linked together.

Logo   A kind of badge or design, usually used by a company or organization.

Middle Ages   The period in Europe from about 800 to 1450.

Patriot   Someone who loves their country and is loyal to it.

Protractor   An instrument used to measure the degrees in a circle or an angle.

Radioactive   Giving off radiation, which can be harmful to human beings.

Sickle   A sharp tool used by farmers to cut grass.

Vowel   One of five letters of the alphabet, a, e, i, o or u.

BOOKS TO READ

Exploring Communications by Cliff Lines (Wayland, 1988)

Flags by Theodore Rowland-Entwistle (Wayland, 1988)

Living With Deafness by Barbara Taylor (Franklin Watts, 1989)

Pocket Book of Flags by Eric Inglefield (Kingfisher, 1988)

DID YOU SOLVE THE PROBLEMS?

How many of the problems could you solve?

Page 5:
1 No Parking
2 Slippery Road Surface
3 Two-way Traffic
4 Hump-backed Bridge
5 Roadworks
6 Children Crossing
7 No U-turns
8 Level Crossing

PICTURE ACKNOWLEDGEMENTS

Barnaby's Picture Library 10, 13 (above), 24; Mary Evans Picture Library 26 (both); Eye Ubiquitous 18, 27; Magdalene College, Cambridge 23; Peter Newark's Western Americana 25; Paul Seheult 6 (right), 22, 28, 29 (all); Tony Stone Worldwide 13; Topham Picture Library 12; Tim Woodcock *cover*; ZEFA 4, 6 (left), 7, 8, 14, 17.

INDEX